World of
CATS

World of
CATS

Howard Loxton

OMEGA BOOKS

Contents

Series edited by Howard Loxton
Picture research by Ann Davies

This edition published 1983 by Omega Books Ltd,
1 West Street, Ware, Hertfordshire, under licence
from the proprietor.

Copyright © 1976 Elsevier Publishing Projects SA, Lausanne.

ISBN 0 907853 24 2

Printed and bound in Hong Kong by South China Printing Co.

Introduction

Is it possible to define what makes the cat such a very attractive animal?
Perhaps for each of us the reasons will differ, and they will differ according to our
own experience of cats. Some people see them as selfish, self-centred and
self-contained and admire their skilful manipulation of circumstances to get
their own way much as they secretly admire the person who makes a wordly success
through unscrupulousness. Others see cats as cuddly bundles of fur, docile and
undemanding. There are those who think a lively kitten is fun, but watch for its
character to change and then lose interest as it grows older. Some will admire
a particular pedigree breed, others the tough cockiness of an alley cat.
Such attitudes probably reveal far more about people than about cats, even if
gained from experience, for despite their much vaunted independence the way
in which cats behave is greatly modified by the way in which they live
and the manner in which they are treated. Cat owners who expect a cat to behave
in a certain way probably end up with just that kind of cat.
Nothing can remove the basic characteristics of the cat. Some cats are
superlatively beautiful, some bear the tattered scars of tough times and hard
fought battles, but all display a sense of style, pride, graceful movement, awareness
and individuality that sets them apart from other animals.
This book sets out in search of cats, the qualities they have in common and the
interest they have as individuals. The words are by a human. In the pictures
the cats tell their own story—cheating sometimes as they do in life.

The Ubiquitous Cat

When you see a noble tiger pacing in his cage at the zoo, or a lion playing with a ball or lying on his back, are you reminded of a tabby cat at home gracefully stretching or rolling over for his tummy to be tickled? It is hardly surprising if you are for the big cats and the domestic cat are very closely related. In fact, the dog, the cat and the bear are all descendants of the same weasel-like animal which lived fifty million years ago. Ten million years of evolution produced an animal very like the modern cat family and from this developed the saber-toothed tiger of the Pleistocene Era (though that line of evolution came to a dead end) and all the modern cats. One of the smaller wildcats eventually evolved into the domestic type, although exactly which no one is very sure. Perhaps different species evolved in different parts of the world: the Spotted Cat in India, the African and European Wildcats in their territories. Mummified cats found during excavations in Egypt proved to be the African Wildcat *Felis lybica*, and since our earliest evidence of domesticated cats comes from Egypt they are generally considered to have been its major ancestor.

The African Wildcat and the European Wildcat are very like a domestic cat in appearance and both can interbreed with domestic cats. The European cat can easily be mistaken for a large feral tabby but a closer look shows that it has a shorter, thicker tail and a stouter head as well as being generally more heavily built. It once lived in wooded lands from Britain across Europe into Asia, though it never crossed the sea to Ireland. Today it is restricted to remote areas where it is seldom disturbed by man. Most of the cats people see and think of as wild are actually feral domestic cats. The cat family are so well matched to their environment and way of life that they have changed little in millions of years. The modern cat was established long before the modern dog but while the dog displays 350, or even more, different breeds the cat has only about 80 recognized varieties, and most of these are only color variations. This is because the cat was the last of the common domestic animals to be domesticated. The dog was man's hunting companion in the remote days of the caveman; fowl and cattle were being raised soon after man began to lead a settled agricultural existence; but it is not until the New Kingdom in Egypt (about 1600 BC) that clear evidence exists of the cat as a domestic animal. Cats appear in connection with man at earlier dates in Egyptian history but there is no way of proving that they had actually been domesticated. Probably cats had found their way into human settlements and into homes long before in search of prey, and because man found them useful to control rodents their presence had been tolerated or even encouraged.

The Egyptians showed great respect and affection for cats. They were venerated as symbols of the gods and it was anathema to harm them. If a cat died its owner went into mourning. There were other animals equally sacred and perhaps modern people, who tend to have a greater affection for the cat than for the crocodile, the ibis, the falcon or the mongoose, exaggerate its position in the religious

hierarchy of ancient Egypt. But it was in cat form that the great god Ra (the Sun) daily overcame the power of darkness in the form of a serpent, named Apep, and it was in the form of a cat that the goddess Bast was represented. At Bubastis, in Lower Egypt, the temple which was the center of her cult was one of the most magnificent in Egypt. In subterranean burial chambers thousands upon thousands of mummified cats were placed by owners who brought them from far away to be interred close to this sacred place. Many owners of Abyssinian cats believe that this breed is directly descended from the cats of ancient Egypt. These elegant cats certainly look very like some of the cats represented in Egyptian paintings and statuettes, but the ticked or "agouti" pattern of their coats can appear naturally as spontaneous mutations in ordinary tabby litters. Their appearance is also like that of the African Wildcat. Although the first Abyssinian in western Europe was recorded as having been taken to Britain in 1868, a picture published a few years later shows it to be totally unlike the modern breed which is almost certainly a creation of British breeders.

Another cat which resembles some of the Egyptian paintings even more closely is the Egyptian Mau, specially created in recent years by both European and American breeders to reproduce the overall appearance and spotted coat of several ancient pictures. The British breeders have added an extra refinement by creating cats in which there is the sign of a scarab beetle—a potent symbol in Egyptian art—appearing in the animal's markings in the center of the forehead, just where such designs are found on some Egyptian cat figures.

The Egyptians tried to prevent the export of their cats but some were smuggled out by Phoenician traders who sailed the length and breadth of the Mediterranean. The Greeks did not give cats much attention, although they do appear in some Greek sculpture, painted on vases and as characters in Aesop's fables which date from the sixth century BC. But by the time of the Roman empire cats, along with exotic Egyptian religions, became fashionable and by the beginning of the Christian era they were frequently kept in smart Roman homes in Italy and in the colonies.

The spread of Christianity and the decline of Egyptian religion

Leopard
Cat

European
Wildcat

Abyssinian
kitten

It is probably in the century following that they were introduced into Japan, although legend dates it several centuries later when the Emperor Ichi-Jo (986-1011) imported a white cat which produced five pure white kittens at the imperial palace in Kyoto.

Some people have suggested that the first Japanese cats must have been taken direct from ancient Egypt because the languages of both cultures use a similar word for the cat—mau—but this is so obviously an onomatopaeic name that all it really shows is that all cats speak a very similar language no matter where they live! (In Egyptian the word also meant "to see", a comment on the cat's keen eyes.) Certainly cats became very popular at the Japanese court and for a time were favorite and highly pampered pets, finding a place in the country's mythology and religion. One cat, kept to protect the manuscripts of a temple from the depredations of mice and rats, devised means of waylaying passers-by and making them visit her lowly temple so that their offerings would make it rich. Now it has become a shrine with a cemetery for cats where Tokyo cat lovers bring offerings and place small cat figures to help their own pets in the after life. Row upon row of painted panels show the original cat, Maneki-Neko, with her paw raised in a gesture of greeting which has become a symbol for good luck. Maneki-Neko and many of the cats which appear in Japanese paintings and prints have a very short tail and a patched coat. This breed, originally known only in Japan, has now been introduced into the Western world and is recognized as a breed by the show organizations of North America.

In other parts of the world other types of cat developed. The European cat was short-haired and cobby-bodied. It is generally supposed that the basic type was tabby, but Flemish paintings sometimes show a gray cat and one English authority describes English cats as of various colors but mainly "griseld, like to congealed ice". The seventeenth century antiquarian John Aubrey says that the common English cat was white patched with bluish gray and that tabbies known as "Cyprus Cats" were not introduced until the 1630s.

led to the abandonment of restrictions on cats being taken out of Egypt, so throughout the Roman territories they began to replace the polecats and ferrets which had been used previously to control vermin.

At about the same time as Aesop was telling his moral tales at the court of King Croesus, a Brahmin philosopher, the equally legendary Pilpay, was using the cat in his Hindu fables. So it is obvious that the cat had, by this time, become a familiar domestic animal in India too.

Chinese art portrays cats as early as 2000 BC but there is no firm indication that they were domestic animals until nearly AD 400.

Tabbies taken to the New World by European settlers on the Eastern seaboard of what is now the United States at some time cross bred with long-haired cats from the orient to produce the fine cat now known as the Maine Coon Cat. Long-haired cats are often known as Persians or Angora cats, both names related to their origin, for it was from Turkey and Iran that the first cats with long hair were taken to Europe. There are no wildcats with long hair so this must have been the result of a mutation that was developed, or at least encouraged, by man.

The Angora, or Ankara cat, named after the capital of Turkey, is actually a distinct type. It has a longer body and tail than the Persian and a smaller head with more upright ears. A few years ago it was in danger of dying out but a careful breeding program was begun at Ankara Zoo to preserve the type. In 1963 a pair were

taken to America and since 1970 it has been a recognized breed in the United States.

Another Turkish cat, developed in the area around Lake Van high in the mountains in the eastern part of that country, is known in the West either as the Turkish Cat or the Van Cat. These attractive and hardy animals—their native territory is under snow for several months of the year—have long white coats with auburn markings. They are sometimes known as Swimming Cats for they really enjoy being in water and swim in the streams of their homeland. A pair were taken to England in 1955 and they have now become a recognized European breed.

Siamese cats are perhaps the best known breed with a national name. Although they are said to have been kept in Thailand for centuries and the Seal Point type was described in a Thai text dating from

Egyptian Mau

Angora

9

Manx

Balinese

◁ Turkish (Van) Cat

Himalayan (Colourpoint) ▷

the Ayddha period (1350-1767), there is no evidence that they originated there. In fact they are not very numerous in Thailand and are sometimes referred to by Thais as Chinese cats. The modern appearance and colors of Siamese breeds are largely the development of European and American breeders.

One cat which is definitely indigenous to Thailand, and is only now becoming known elsewhere, is the silver-blue coated Korat, which the Thais call the *Si-Sawat* (sawat means good luck). In remote villages they are said to act as "watchdogs" and the males are reputed to be pugnacious defenders. Europeans have found that they make delightful pets. A blue-coated cat from Malaya is thought to have had some part in the Korat's ancestry. Another blue cat was found by missionary monks in South Africa who took it back to France

to create the breed now known as the Chartreux after the Carthusian monks who introduced it.

The Russian Blue, despite the fact that is was once known as the Archangel Cat, did not necessarily come from Russia; tailless cats like the Manx occur in many places other than the Isle of Man; the Havana has nothing to do with Cuba; the Himalayan was produced in Britain (where it is known as the Colourpoint) and the Balinese in North America. The Burmese, however, did probably originate in Burma; the Cornish and Devon Rex do stem from cats discovered in those English counties and the German Rex is descended from a mutation discovered in Berlin.

Cat fanciers throughout the world are continually developing new color varieties and crosses between existing breeds, which they hope

will eventually be recognized as official breeds. Others are carefully ensuring the preservation of the characteristics of the already acknowledged breeds. But, whether a cat is an expensive pedigree breed or an unaristocratic mongrel, it will share the feline qualities which make the cat such a well-loved and attractive pet and to its owner it will have an individual appeal which makes it a cat among cats.

How far has the domestic cat changed from its wild relations? Very little. Without the artificial breeding control exercised by owners, feral cats are said to revert within a few generations to the tabby coat of their ancestors. Every cat is more or less able to survive in the wild, according to the degree of dependence which has been developed in it; although a cat that has never learned to kill its prey will become a scavanger rather than a predator. Nevertheless, the fact that cats can fend for themselves is no reason for forcing them to do so. Our cities have very large cat populations and, since so many humans lack a sense of responsibility for their pets, many are homeless strays. Sometimes they will live solitary and

independent lives; sometimes—as for instance in the Forum in Rome—they will form a feral colony. Often such colonies will be fed by cat lovers who ensure that they do not starve during the privations of winter. Although they will accept the food or milk which is left for them and their ever-increasing litters of kittens, there is no easy way in which they can be treated for any sickness and, unless they are captured and neutered, there is no way of controlling their numbers apart from hunger and disease. We need cats to be active rodent exterminators and do not want them all to spend their lives on silken cushions, but the large feral populations in our over cat-populated cities are in danger of becoming reservoirs of disease. Even the cat that never goes outside the house is susceptible to the scourges of cat flu and feline infectious enteritis (panleucopenia), which frequently can be lethal and is always critical. Such viral infections and other germs can be brought in on your shoes and clothing, and that of your visitors, human or animal. The housebound cat, unexposed to the wide range of minor infections which are always present has less chance to built up antibodies than the cat

which can range free. It is vitally important that all cats are regularly immunized against panleucopenia and a careful record kept of when booster doses are required. Any stray which you adopt, or new cat which you acquire, should be taken to the vet to be given a rigorous medical check. If you suspect that your cat may have an infectious cat disease do not take it straight to the veterinarian's surgery. Telephone first: the vet may prefer to make a visit to your home, to arrange an appointment out of surgery hours, or ask you to use a special entrance to his office to avoid contact with other cats. Unless you have decided that you want to breed, and are prepared to be responsible for any kittens, neutering of cats should be an automatic decision for all owners of domestic pets. It is impossible to control the sex life of adult cats unless they are locked up and deprivation of mating can have serious affects on their health. Neutering is the only sensible way of avoiding unwanted kittens. It is a very simple operation for males. Although spaying a female requires major surgery it is an operation carried out many times a week by most vets and no cause for worry or concern. When you take a new cat for its first medical check up discuss the best time for the operation with your vet and plan ahead. If you own a tom it is your duty to your neighbors to have it neutered and will avoid unpleasant spraying about your own house. If you have a queen remember that she can still be safely spayed after allowing her to have such litters as you decide you are prepared to rear. It is always better to subject your cat to a small operation than to be responsible for the putting down of unwanted kittens.

The Sensual Cat

Can you see as well as your cat? Or hear so clearly, smell as keenly, move as quickly or spring as sharply? If you have senses as aware and a physique as well controlled as your cat you should have no difficulty in collecting an Olympic medal, provided that you have no aspirations to being the winner of the marathon or a long distance track event.

Physically the cat is very like a human being and has a very similar brain—for that reason it is widely used as an experimental animal and more is known about the cat's brain than that of any other animal. In most respects a cat is far better physically equipped than man and is physically superior to most other mammals. What a cat lacks is stamina.

The cat is geared to a life in which bursts of intense activity alternate with periods of complete stillness and repose. It will beat you in a race over any short distance (you will rarely catch a cat that has not tacitly agreed to being caught). But go for a reasonably paced walk over a couple of miles and it will be exhausted before you have been out for more than half an hour. This is because the cat's heart and lungs are small compared with its overall body size and cannot support sustained activity. Like other carnivorous animals, which are never quite sure where their next meal is coming from or when it will be, they need a large stomach and digestive system to enable them to gorge themselves when they have made a kill and then be able to go for long periods of fasting. The digestive organs take up space and prevent the heart and lungs from being larger. In one other way the cat cannot excel us: it does not see in such rich and varied color as we do. At one time it was thought that cats could not distinguish color at all. The surface of our retina is made up of rods, which register light intensity, and cones, which register color. We have a ratio of six times as many cones to rods compared with the ratio in the cat. But what the cat therefore lacks in color perception it gains in sensitivity to light. The light passing through the cat's eye is also reflected back by a mirror-like layer known as the tapetum lucidum which further increases its light sensitivity. The tapetum, which is responsible for the red eye shine seen in a number of nocturnal animals if their eyes catch the light, enables light which has passed through the eye to have a second chance of activating the retinal cells on its return journey. The extra proportion of rods and the tapetum give the cat a brightness discrimination seven times better than that of a human.

The cat can also control the size of the iris of its eye, the aperture which regulates light entering. It can be reduced to a narrow vertical slit to cut down the amount of light and avoid dazzle in bright light, at the same time giving deeper focus (like narrowing the aperture in a camera). The iris can be enlarged to a full round circle in dark conditions to enable every possible glimmer of light to register. The cat cannot see in real darkness—no animal can—but it can see under conditions which we would find impossible to register. The cat's hearing also ranges far beyond the limits of our own: from thirty cycles to forty-five thousand cycles per second.

Its optimum range extends as far as eight thousand cycles (four thousand further than man's) and there is no appreciable falling off until forty thousand. In addition its ears are ridged and shaped to concentrate the sound that falls upon them and can be moved in all directions. The cat can turn its head almost completely around to catch a noise from any direction.

The sense of smell is also very acute. Scent information plays an important part in marking territories, sexual signaling, food location and all kinds of identification. Taste seems to have little importance in the wild and this is not a very highly developed sense, although individual cats show marked preferences for certain foods.

Every part of a cat's body is highly sensitive to touch. The slightest pressure on a single hair can produce a reaction because the body is scattered with tiny raised areas which send an immediate signal

to the nervous system. The cat also has a number of ultrasensitive hairs, chiefly the whiskers, eyebrows, long cheek hairs and long hairs on the back of its wrists, which seem to react not only to direct contact but also to changes in pressure about them, enabling the cat to recognize the presence of objects by the minute changes of pressure which they create in the air around them. This, not the width of the whiskers, is how a cat judges whether a hole is large enough to go through in the dark. A cat with damaged or missing whiskers will usually show poor spatial judgement.

Such a sophisticated sensory system enables the cat to collect and interpret information quickly and accurately, but it would be of little value were it not linked with a beautifully engineered physique. The cat's skeleton is extremely flexible and its muscles are powerful and can take great strain. A cat can jump up on to a wall many times its own height—compare your own size with that of a cat and think how high you would have to leap to cover a comparable distance—it can spring with incredible accuracy across space and can maintain its balance in awkward circumstances. The balance mechanisms of the inner ear are not properly understood but the simple fact that cats—unlike dogs and human beings— are neither car, air or sea-sick shows that some difference must exist. The cat's uncanny ability to right itself while falling and make a perfect four-point landing depends on more than just the labyrinthine canals of the inner ear. Their vision helps orientation by providing a "horizon". Experiments with a cat born without

the balance organs of the ear showed that it failed to right itself when dropped blindfolded. Although a cat will usually right itself this does not mean that it will always avoid injury for a fall may result in a greater impact on touching the ground than its muscles can cushion; it may break a limb, or it may catch its jaw and fracture the jaw bone or split the palate. Sometimes a cat dreaming in a deep sleep may move in response to its dream and fall from a ledge on which it is lying not rousing itself in time to right itself— good reason for discouraging your cat from sunning itself on external window ledges unless they are equipped with rails to stop it falling over.

The domestic cat does not usually have to seek out a living and if overfed may become overweight and lethargic; the fault then lies with the owner and not the cat. Most pet cats prefer a lively life and enjoy testing their skills and reactions whenever they have the opportunity. Even in repose they take enormous delight in sensual pleasures. Basking in sunshine or stretched out in front of a blazing fire, they love warmth. Stroking, massage, tickling— even scratching—will produce a satisfied purr, the cat's sure indication of pleasure. If the stimulating hand is directed to the wrong part of the body they will often maneuver themselves or push the hand with their paw to change its location. Some cats show a definite taste in music, which must be entirely a sensual appreciation for it can have little connection with their natural instincts. Although their pleasure in watching the world is largely an expression of their

inquisitive nature, their occasional preference for certain television programs suggests a more aesthetic appreciation. (In one pair of household cats from the same litter one showed a marked enthusiasm for classical ballet while the other preferred a popular Western series!)

Smells seem to give cats enormous pleasure. Many cats become delirious with delight at the scent of the plant known as catnip or catmint (*Nepeta cataria*) and cat toys are often stuffed with it. Siamese, however, often show indifference to it and young kittens tend to avoid the plant until they are about three months old. Cat thyme (*Teucrium marum*), valerian, patchouli and matatabi are also plants to which cats seem particularly attracted (although matatabi has no apparent smell for humans). They like the scent of many fragrant flowers and enjoy the smell of some man-made perfumes although individual cats will show their own preferences. They will also take enormous pleasure in scents which we would find repugnant. This is partly because scent carries a great deal of information for a cat and a sniffing investigation of the smells carried by a returning human or animal friend will be like a good gossip about where they have been and what they have done.

You will often find a cat sitting with its mouth open and a look of what appears to be extreme distaste upon its face. It is actually exactly the opposite, for the cat so likes or is so intrigued by a particular smell that it has detected that it has opened its mouth to increase the intake of air and enable more of the odor to be collected by its olfactory cells.

Cats also make an important use of scent by marking their own territory with secretions from their scent glands. Males mark territory by spraying urine, and even neutered toms may continue to do so if the practice has already become firmly established before they are altered. All cats will leave their scent on places that they particularly claim as their own, such as a sleeping basket or a special chair, and it is believed that when they rub their heads against a friendly human hand they are actually leaving an identifying scent

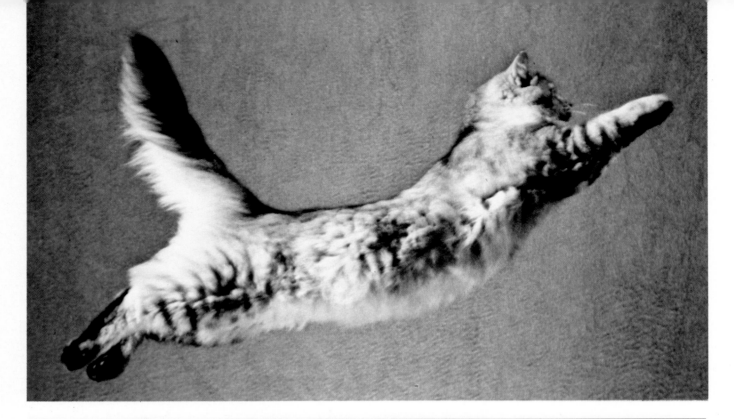

which is secreted by glands found on their cheeks.

The mature female coming into season will notify her readiness to mate to neighborhood males through a scent message strong enough to be interpreted over a considerable distance. She will also make characteristic mating calls which can be quite raucous in the Siamese, although some females seem to be able to supress this instinctive vocalization in the hope that their owners will not realize that they are on heat and will still allow them to go in and out. Indeed, some cats have produced kittens without their owners having the slightest idea that they were to be expected—but they are the exception. Most females make it quite clear that they are ready to mate and you will probably find toms lining up outside the house if you do not let the female out. Naturally, if you are keeping a pedigree cat for breeding purposes you will want to control its matings, but persistently

preventing a mature cat from mating can lead to serious health and psychological problems. So, unless you are prepared to accept an increase in the cat population in your own household or know that you have good homes waiting for any resulting litters, it would be much better to have a pet female spayed (and you can always have this done after she has borne a litter).

Cats have a centuries-old reputation for being highly sexed— indeed, in some languages "cat" has been used as a term for a prostitute—but there is no reason to suppose that they are more sexually active than other mammals. The female cat, however, does take a much more active part in courtship than is the case with most animals, and whether from purely instinctive processes or an awareness of pleasure in the act they will make every possible effort to find their way out to a mate if you try to prevent them from

doing so. A door left temporarily ajar or a slightly opened window will be watched for avidly. That is not to say that any tom will do. Females can be extremely selective in deciding which mates they will accept. Sometimes there may be an apparent love match with other males being rejected; on other occasions an orgy has been known to develop which could go on for several days, resulting in a cat bearing a litter of kittens by different fathers.

The cat is an extremely fastidious animal. Its motto might well be, "If in doubt, then wash". It will often break off in the middle of some other activity to make some adjustment to its toilette. Although immediately after a thorough grooming cats will sometimes roll around in dust and dirt, they cannot bear not to be clean and if sickness prevents them from keeping their coat clean and well groomed this has a very bad effect on their morale and can seriously hamper their recovery. Help with grooming is an important part of nursing sick or elderly cats.

The cat's long, rough-surfaced tongue acts both as wash rag and comb. It can reach almost every part of the body except the head and back of the neck. To reach them it uses its paw as a sponge, wetting it first with its tongue and then rubbing away at head and ears to keep them clean. Cats seem to positively enjoy washing themselves and gain from it something far more than the satisfaction of being clean. Perhaps it gives them the same sense of relaxation as some humans achieve by indulging in a hot bath.

The Necessary Cat

When the ancient Egyptians visualized their sun god taking the form of a cat to vanquish night in the shape of a serpent each and every dawn were they transferring to myth what was already an observed occurrence in their daily lives? Snakes seem to have a fascination for cats and it is said that cats will play with them, dead or alive, and that they often become skilled in killing them— yet there is little evidence that cats ever eat snakes. Diodorus of Sicily, writing in the first century before Christ, mentions the usefulness of cats in killing snakes. Could it be that, centuries before, the Egyptians were already keeping cats to free their homes of dangerous snakes? This seems a worthy and important role for a sacred animal, but Egypt was *the* great grain producing country of its time and cats would also have been invaluable in protecting the contents of its granaries.

Towards the end of the fourth century of the Christian era, Palladius, a writer on agricultural topics, recommended cats to deal with moles damaging artichoke beds. It was certainly their use to control mice and rats that eventually earned the cat a place in the homesteads of Europe. Sometimes an exact cash value was put upon the cat to match its abilities. During the ninth century it was decreed by Henry I of Saxony that anyone who killed an adult cat should be fined sixty bushels of corn. In Wales a century later the Dimetian code declared:

"The worth of a cat that is killed or stolen: its head to be put downward upon a clean even floor, with its tail lifted upwards, and thus suspended, whilst wheat is poured about it until the tip of its tail be covered; and that is to be its worth. If the corn cannot be had then a milch sheep, with her lamb and wool, is its value, if it be a cat which guards the king's barn.

"The worth of a common cat is four legal pence (after it shall kill mice)."

"Whosoever shall sell a cat is to answer for her not going a caterwauling every moon; and that she devour not her kittens, and that she have ears, teeth and nails, and be a good mouser."

Under the laws of Hywel Dda, Prince of South Wales, issued about AD 940 it was decreed:

"This is the complement of a lawful hamlet: nine buildings and one plough and one churn and one cat and one cock and one bull and one herdsman."

But there were those who did not think the cat so useful or so necessary. Its important place in Egyptian religion and its connection with some of the Nordic gods caused the fathers of the early Church to decry the cat as an agent of the devil. Although folk superstitions sometimes still reflected the power of the cat—such as killing a cat as the last sheaf of corn was reaped to ensure the next year's fertility, giving the cat the role of the sacrificial god-king of ancient times,

the middle ages saw a strengthening of the belief that cats, especially black ones, had a close link with the devil. As the French *L'Evangile du Diable* puts it "Only fools do not know that all cats have a pact with the Devil ... It is clear why cats sleep, or feign sleep, all day long, by the fire in winter or the sun in summer. Their task is to keep watch in the barns and stables through the night, to see all, to hear all. It is easy to see why the Evil Spirits, warned just in time, always manage to disappear before we can see them."

At Aix-en-Provence each Corpus Christi Day during the middle ages the Church itself led a strangely contradictory ceremony in which a tomcat, wrapped like a baby in tight swaddling bands, was displayed to the people then, at exactly noon, cast into a fire and publicly burned. There is an obvious link with sun worship yet the cat is wrapped like the young Christ Child. We do not know how the priests interpreted this pagan based ceremony but clearly they saw it as consigning evil to the flames as in the burning of a heretic. In Paris too, at midsummer, it was the custom to burn a barrel or sack of live cats which was hung from a pole over the middle of a bonfire in the Place de Grève. At Armentières cats were also burned; at Store Magleby, near Copenhagen, on the eve of Shrove Tuesday, a live cat was shut into a cask at which riders used to tilt; at Ypres cats used to be thrown from the belfry at an annual festival and at Metz thirteen cats used to be burned alive in a wooden cage on the eve of the festival of Saint John.

The Metz burnings commemorated an outbreak of Saint Vitus' dance in 1344 which miraculously ended when a knight, newly arrived in the town, saw an enormous black cat sitting in the hearth of his lodging just as he was about to fall asleep. He made the sign of the cross and drew his sword and the cat disappeared. The knight and the city authorities agreed that it must have been the devil. It became common for the Church to accuse those who were massacred as heretics, such as the Waldensians and Albigensians during the twelfth and thirteenth centuries, of taking part in rites which involved cats. When the Order of the Knights Templar was supressed at the beginning of the fourteenth century, its members confessed to worshipping the devil in the form of a black cat. Nevertheless

the whole Church did not condemn the cat. The rules for an order of anchoresses in Ireland forbade them to keep any animal "but Kat one," and bestiaries written by monkish scholars show that cats' usefulness was recognized in monasteries and abbeys.

In 1484 Pope Innocent VII dealt the cat its greatest blow, denouncing the innocent cat and all who harbored it with effects that were disastrous for man because without cats the number of rats in Europe multiplied unchecked and when the plague came rats carried it everywhere.

Eventually the appreciation of the cat's usefulness gained ground. The cat itself was reinstated as chief rodent exterminator and its importance as a domestic pet began to grow. The cat's delightful qualities as a companion make it an excellent pet for lonely people, but in the seventeenth century a surge of witch hunting began which resulted in many old ladies being tortured and killed because they were devoted to their cats. In stories of the supernatural witches are frequently credited with a supernatural servant or companion. In England they were more particularly considered to have animal "familiars"—minor devils who served them in animal form— not necessarily that of a cat: they might be toads, dogs or any small creature. But it is the cat, and especially the black cat, which has stayed in people's imagination. The English witch hunts found their counterpart on the other side of the Atlantic, most notoriously in the village of Salem in Massachusetts, where one of the witch trial witnesses described how "there came in at the window

the likeness of a cat, which fell upon him, took fast hold of his throat, lay on him a considerable while, and almost killed him."

When he called on the names of the Trinity it "left him, leap'd on the floor and flew out at the window." Even today stories and motion pictures about the occult often feature a black cat as a representative or instrument of the devil.

In contrast to the European situation it was because cats were so highly thought of that vermin got out of hand in Japan. Cats were originally valued because they controlled the mice which ate silkworms and protected grain from rats. When cats became a prized possesssion of the Imperial Court it became fashionable to keep them closely so that breeding could be controlled; they were never allowed to run free and chase prey but were pampered and exercised on leashes. In consequence the silk industry became seriously endangered and grainstores were overrun with vermin. The situation grew so critical that in 1602 a law was passed that all cats should be liberated and heavy fines were imposed on anyone found buying or selling cats.

It is not only on land that the cat has proved a valuable protector of food stores. Every ship needs its cat to keep down rats and there are many tales about them from the true story of the cat of the *Fila Cavena*, which fell overboard and valiantly kept swimming after it, to the legendary cat belonging to Dick Whittington which not only freed his ship of rats but cleared a south sea island of them too.

Japanese sailors, in particular, had faith in the good luck brought
by having a cat aboard, especially if it was a tortoiseshell. They
believed that a cat would be able to foretell the coming of storms
and if sent to the top of the mast would be able to frighten the storm
demons away.

Ship's cats have helped to spread various types of cat around the globe.
The Pilgrim fathers, sailing in the *Mayflower* to their new life
in America, and colonists to new lands in every part of the world
have taken cats with them to help protect their precious stores of grain
and seeds and have adopted kittens born on shipboard. These cats
formed the domestic cat populations in newly settled territories.

Shops, warehouses, factories, restaurants, museums, churches, theatres,
farms—the cat stands guard in them all. Sometimes a stray adopted
by the workpeople or a caretaker, sometimes a cat introduced
especially: they are each in a very real sense public servants—
a role frequently given official recognition—many an official cat's
keep is included in the budget of a government department.

In aiding man the cat has proved itself not only useful but also heroic.
During the long and gruelling seige of Stalingrad (now renamed
Volgograd) during World War II a cat called Mourka carried
messages concerning gun emplacements from a group of scouts
to their company headquarters.

William Shakespeare, whose writings show no evidence of affection
for the cat—unlike the work of so many artists and poets—
described the animal as "the harmless, necessary cat", and both
indeed it is. Harmless to all except man's enemies (although it may
catch a butterfly or kill an occasional bird, birds rarely form more
than an infinitesimal portion of their diet) and very, very useful.

The Predatory Cat

All cats are carnivores. From domestic tabby to ten-foot tiger they need a diet of meat and to find it must catch and kill other animals —unless they can find a ready supply which human beings have killed for them. Opening a can may not seem like murder to many of us but an animal had to die to provide that meat and if you are squeamish about your cat catching the occasional bird or mouse then you had best not have a cat at all. Perhaps, one day, we may see soya bean and other vegetable proteins, which are being developed to provide synthetic meat to ease the world's increasing food problems, used in pet foods but it will take many more centuries of domestication to alter the natural habits and diet pattern of the domestic cat.
Its instincts compel it to chase and to try to catch the small rodents, birds, insects and other creatures which form its natural prey.
It was the cat's efficiency as a mouser and ratter that earned it a welcome place in our homes; its patience and skill in catching prey is something to be wondered at rather than criticized.
Thousands and thousands of years ago the cat evolved into a sophisticated and carefully balanced organism in which brain, sensory system and muscles together produced a skilled and superbly equipped hunter. Sharp eyes, which detect the slightest movement, acute ears which can hear the shrill squeals of mice and identify the source of any sound, and a highly developed sense of smell enable the cat to locate its prey and its soft paws and perfectly controlled movement enable it to approach it stealthily.
The cat can display immeasurable patience, watching a trail along which it is sure its prey will come or stationing itself outside a hole into which a mouse has disappeared and waiting for it to emerge. From such stillness the cat can spurt into violent movement, accelerating rapidly to give chase or leaping with uncanny accuracy to grasp the prey in teeth or claws.
Watch a cat out hunting. If it thinks that prey—or danger—may be near, it makes great use of camouflage, shade and cover; it checks the lie of the land at each corner; it flattens its ears to make it less noticeable when it looks over a wall or ridge. Indoors or outdoors a cat will halt frequently to take stock of the situation. Sniffing for new scent signals, ears pricked for the slightest rustle, freezing, one paw in the air, to avoid being observed.
It moves easily in well-spaced cover, slowly and stealthily when not so well hidden or when less careful movement might make noise, then suddenly dashes across unconcealed ground, melting back into cover again. From your vantage point you may be able to see the cat quite easily—but it is not you that the cat is trying to surprise and from its prey's position the cat will only be noticed by the very alert. Perhaps they will hear it and be put on their guard.
The cat's soft pads make its footfalls soundless to most human ears but no animal can move completely silently. Perhaps the tiny flick at the end of the cat's tail will reveal its location. This is one excited movement that the cat seems unable to supress but even that has been interpreted by some observers as a way of making prey watch the tail tip and ignore the rest of the cat.

When prey has been located the cat first crouches, then runs towards it, keeping the body close to the ground. When it gets closer —the distance being determined by the cover available—the cat pauses, still keeping low, its forepaws flat to the ground and taking most of its weight, its ears pricked forward to catch every sound, whiskers spread and eyes fixed on the prey. For some moments the cat concentrates on following every movement then, if the prey is still some distance away, the procedure may be repeated to get closer or, if it is not so far off, the cat will stalk it slowly and cautiously, getting as close as cover will allow, then halt and prepare to make the "kill".
The weight is now transferred from the pad of the foot on to the toes, the hind legs are moved backwards and may be alternately lifted from the ground, or the weight moved from one to the other, the tail is usually extended and the tip twitches with anticipation. The final attack is most frequently a short, low run; the final spring a thrust forward with the back feet staying on the ground— although a full leap does sometimes precede the kill. By keeping its hind feet on the ground the cat maintains stability if there should be a struggle.
The actual kill is usually made by a firm bite on the back of the neck. If the bite severs the cervical spinal cord or the hind brain, death is almost instantaneous. If the animal is not immediately killed

this is the position which gives the cat the greatest control over it
for the ensuing fight.

These techniques are particularly suited to hunting small rodents,
although if a cat is keeping watch from an elevated position
it will not need to stalk but will spring on to its prey when it reaches
the most convenient position below. If a cat has been watching a hole
or burrow it will not spring as soon as the prey emerges, but
wait concealed until it has got well clear of the burrow and unable
to save itself by a quick dash back down its hole. Hunting birds
in this way is not so effective; they are very likely to fly off before
the cat has completed its ritual of "ambushing" procedures.
In fact, cats are often not good at catching birds, although some
individuals excel at it, having learned to supress the initial stages
of their hunting pattern by staying motionless in cover until a bird
comes close enough to catch.

Flies and butterflies, favorite prey for urban domestic cats, who may
not have much rodent life available and of whom local birds are all
too well aware, settle for longish periods and give a cat an excellent
opportunity to use its classic hunting technique. They will either strike
the insect with a paw or catch it in their mouth. It is amazing
how accurate most cats are with such comparatively small targets.
Bumble bees, larger in size and usually slower moving, seem to be
a favorite with some cats who seem untroubled by a sting on chin
or paw. Most cats learn to avoid both bees and wasps after having
been stung once or twice. If your cat should sustain a sting on
its tongue or in its mouth, the swelling may cause breathing problems
and treatment by your vet should be sought.
A cat watching a fly or a bird which is out of reach on the other side
of a window pane or high in a tree often makes a machine-gun-like
chattering sound which sounds like an explosion of frustration.

They will sometimes make the same sound when potential prey is within easy reach, so can the sound be interpreted as a kind of challenge?

Cats which are deprived of outdoor hunting will use the same hunting patterns when chasing token or toy prey, making use of the cover that furniture and household objects offer. They will even adopt the stalking and attack procedure when approaching prey against a bare floor with no cover whatever; when deprived of real or substitute prey, they will stalk inanimate objects or even totally imaginary creatures.

Although all cats seem instinctively to chase after small moving objects, the technique of killing does not seem to be an instinctive and is certainly not linked directly with food among domestic pets which may have been prevented from learning to kill prey in kittenhood. Research conducted by P. Leyhausen showed that the properly placed neck bite usually first occurs when a mother brings in live prey for her kittens (when they are $2^1/2$ to 3 months old). A considerable degree of excitement has to be developed before a kill is made, for a kitten must overcome its trepidation at the unknown behavior of what might be dangerous prey. Competition with litter mates usually provides this, but it can be set off by human competition and it can also be built up by prolonged play with the animal.

"For when he takes his prey he plays with it to give it a chance. For one mouse in seven escapes by his dallying . . ." says Christopher Smart in his famous poem about his cat Jeffery, but initially it was the cat reassuring itself—rather than intentionally giving the mouse a sporting chance—that resulted in this pattern of action. The kitten, anxious lest the mouse should do it harm, will release it momentarily, although still keeping overall control of its movements, until it has worked itself up sufficiently to make

the kill. The same behavior persists in the adult cat even when
it has become an experienced killer. Sometimes a difficult fight
with prey will excite the cat so much that its behavior does not change
when it has made the kill and it will persistently throw the prey
into the air and catch it until the excitement has been dissipated.
In the wild carnivorous animals do not eat only the fleshy part
of their kill. They eat the stomach contents of their herbivorous prey
and thus obtain useful vitamins, especially vitamin B complex
which is produced by fermentation in the stomach. (Big cats will start
their meal by slitting open an animal's stomach, but the domestic cat
will usually commence eating from the head.) In feeding domestic
cats, proprietary foods can often be purchased which are formulated
to supply all the necessary dietary ingredients. Cats fed on meat
or fish should be given calcium or vitamin supplements, or encouraged
to eat vegetables, cereals and bone meal if they will, to make up
any deficiencies.

Cow's milk will supply calcium but some cats will not drink it—
and it certainly plays no part in a wildcat's diet—even if a cat
drinks milk always remember to have fresh water available,
especially if you feed your cat dry foods which, although very
convenient, may increase any tendency to urinary troubles in cats
which do not drink a great deal. Another essential is to make sure
that a cat has access to grass. Partly because of the fur which they
swallow when washing themselves, and perhaps because they may eat
some of the fur or feathers of their prey, cats produce balls of fur
which can cause a blockage in their digestive tracts. Eating grass
acts as a natural emetic and helps them to bring hairballs up.
They also seem to eat grass when generally out of sorts, so it
probably has other medicinal effects as well. If your cat has no
outdoor source of grass readily available then you should grow some
in a pot indoors.

The Maternal Cat

Sharing the experience of the birth and rearing of a litter of kittens is a fascinating and rewarding experience for any cat owner— but not one to be undertaken unless you are able to accommodate perhaps another half dozen cats in your own household or have definite promises of homes for them. If you have a pedigree cat and have it mated to a well-chosen stud you will probably not have so much difficulty in disposing of your kittens. Unless you plan to become a cat breeder, think very carefully before deciding to let your cat have kittens for the litter's future is your responsibility. If you have a female cat and have not had it spayed, a litter is a responsibility which you may well find yourself forced to accept. It is the unusual and the difficult which tends to attract most attention in life: you may have heard stories of emergency caesarean births and kittens that prove difficult to rear. They are the exception and most female cats find giving birth something which they take easily in their stride. Cats usually make capable and dutiful mothers. However, in case any difficulties should develop every cat owner with an expectant female should be well informed on what to expect and how to help.

Most cats seem to be extremely highly sexed and if you have no objection to a mongrel litter your cat will probably find her own mate without any help from you. Such random mating will not allow you to have any control over the kittens' appearances, or their genetic inheritance of weaknesses or sickness. A planned mating will enable you to chose a tom to improve any weakness in your queen (as female cats are known in the Cat Fancy) to preserve her fine points and to ensure a healthy line. If both cats are properly registered the kittens will have official pedigrees. If they are registered, in turn they will become more valuable. Keeping a stud-tom and making all the necessary provisions for a controlled mating is an expensive business. You will have to pay a stud fee for a pedigree mating, but few cat breeders are out to make big profits (indeed, for most it probably works out a very expensive hobby) and this will not usually be very high considering the trouble involved. The breeder from whom you first got your cat or the local vet's receptionist will probably be able to help you find a suitable stud, or you will be able to trace one with the help of the breed society whose address you can get from national Cat Fancy organizations. Find your tom well before your queen is due to come on heat and discuss the necessary arrangements with his owner so that the mating can be fixed at very short notice when she is in season. How long she will stay with the tom and how many matings take place will vary according to practice at the stud you chose. If conception does not take place many stud owners will arrange a further mating

to feel them—but do not try squeezing the cat or you may do it harm. As the foeti develop their mother will want extra food—you will know when for she will ask for it! Vary her diet, keeping it well balanced, and if you wish give vitamin and mineral supplements but do not overfeed.

As a pregnant cat approaches her time she may gather material to make a nest, like one queen who found a roll of upholstery stuffing and tore off pieces until she was discovered. She will certainly be thinking about a quiet place to have her kittens. Unless you want her to disappear to have them on her own—a working cat with little human contact may well do this but a well-loved cat will probably be proud to involve you in the birth—it would be sensible to do some thinking yourself. Decide upon a warm, draft-free place, protected from strong light and away from the disturbance of day-to-day domestic activity, but easily accessible and clear of potential dangers for mother or kittens. Prepare a nesting box, a cardboard box with bedding of torn-up newspaper covered with a towel will serve, and put it where you want her to have her kittens. Encourage her to use it before they are due so that she impregnates it with her scent creating an easily identified home base for her kittens when they arrive. If she seems determined to prepare a nest somewhere else it will be simpler to move the box to the location she has chosen (provided that it is not somewhere totally unsuitable) than to try to change her mind.

The mother will probably become excessively affectionate shortly before the litter is due. Her nipples may show a trace of milk and there may be a slight exudation from her vulva. Now is the time to put another piece of cloth in the kittening box to keep the other bedding clean. Move her litter tray within an easy distance so that she, and the kittens, when they are old enough, do not have to far to go. If the cat is closely involved with you she will probably come and let you know when she feels labor about to begin. Some cats prefer to disappear and emerge when everything is over. The natural behavior of the cat family is to seek solitude for their parturition, but many domestic pets are delighted to have close humans at hand. For these cats the security given by human company seems greater than that given by safe seclusion; they may even refuse to stay in their chosen kittening place if they are deserted. However, if a cat is not normally very trusting, or you do not know it well, do not intrude or interfere for she may mistake your helpful intentions for a threat. Motherhood can make a cat agressive, especially to strangers, and frightened cats have been known to turn on their own kittens.

without charge, but they are not bound to do this (there are few occasions when fertilization does not succeed). If a queen persistently does not conceive it is best to consult your vet for she may have some gynecological disorder.

Cats produce their kittens about sixty-four days after conception but this may vary a little either way. If their owner or a favorite human is away from home they may sometimes, somehow, delay labor for a few days until his or her return.

It is not noticeable that a cat is pregnant until some weeks after mating. At about three weeks the nipples may appear very pink and after a month they may begin to swell, but these indications could easily go unobserved if you did not know that the cat had been mated. A vet should be able to confirm that embryos are developing at this stage and an experienced breeder may be able

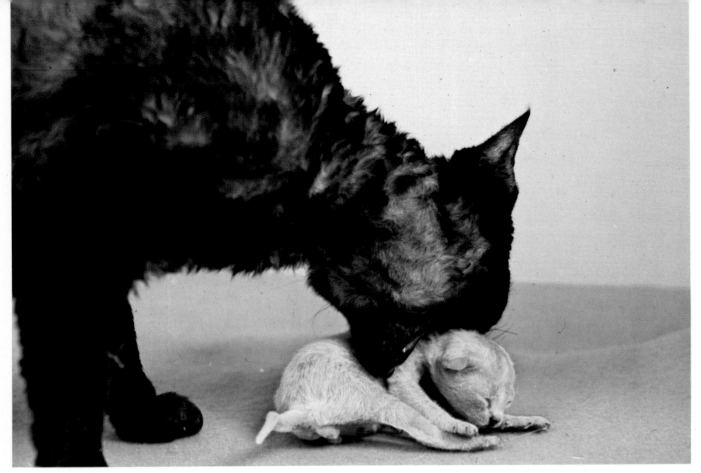

Seeing an animal born is a thrilling experience. It is not a pretty sight to watch, but it is a moving one. Most cats know exactly what to do and as soon as a kitten is delivered will break the sac and begin to wash the kitten and to encourage it to breathe, bite through the umbilical cord and eat the placenta. If you are present at the birth of kittens, check that a placenta is delivered for each kitten, for should one remain within the mother it could lead to difficulties and possible infection later. If she is a first-time mother the cat may not be quite sure what to do, or perhaps the kittens may follow each other too quickly for her to cope, and your help may save their lives. It is easy to tear the sac open with your fingers, clear it from the kitten's mouth and begin to clean the kitten with a damp, rough piece of towel. If the kitten does not begin to breathe apply artificial respiration straight away. If you should lose a kitten do not waste time getting upset, concentrate on helping with the rest of the litter.

Have fresh water nearby for when the mother gets thirsty and put out some food for her. When all the kittens have been born and cleaned she may need some, indeed she may take a little between births, and she will also want a quiet rest.

Kittens may begin to suckle within half an hour of birth but often this will be delayed until parturition is complete. The new-born pushes itself forward with its back legs, all the time moving its head from side to side, until it finds its mother, and muzzles against her to locate a nipple.

For the next twelve hours the mother will stay with her kittens almost continuously, suckling them and resting. For a further two days she will spend almost all her time with them. Then she will begin to leave them for short periods, usually well under an hour. When they are left on their own the kittens will huddle together to keep warm. On her return their mother will wash them vigorously to wake them and to start them feeding. She will curl herself around them, both to control their movement and to help them find her nipples.

Most cats make excellent mothers but occasionally one may reject her kittens. If this should happen, or if they should be orphaned or their mother be too weak to rear them all, you must either find a foster mother or hand rear them yourself. This is a time-consuming task but not a difficult one. They have to be kept warm, fed regularly with milk made to a formula which closely resembles cat's milk and cleaned and massaged to keep their digestive system working. If you are not experienced with kittens seek the advice of your vet or an established breeder. Kittens which never suckle from their mother do not receive the special colostrum rich milk which in their first day provides them with antibodies against many forms of disease.

Apart from removing the soiled top bedding after kittening is over do not disturb the mother and her young kittens more than necessary. Visitors should wait to see the new family until they have opened their eyes at about ten days old. Until then they will suckle

and sleep and do not usually wander from the nest until they are two weeks old. If they manage to make an occasional foray away from their mother they will be promptly rounded up. If their mother is worried by noise or too much going on in their vicinity she may even pick them up and carry them, one by one, to somewhere more private that she thinks a safer spot. A cat with her first litter will instinctively try to pick them up in her mouth but, at first, she may take hold of any part of them—only experiment teaches her that the easiest way is to grip them by the scruff of the neck. There is nothing more bedraggled looking than a new-born kitten, but within hours of birth kittens will have begun to change their appearance, their coats being dry will make a lot of difference in itself. They will soon begin to fill out and should put on weight rapidly and regularly. Weigh them on the kitchen scales (take the scales to them and not them to the scales) and keep a note of how heavy they are each day. A newborn kitten should gain about 10 gram (1/3 ounce) during the first day and rather more thereafter. If there is no increase, or even a drop, in weight you should consult your vet.

If there is anything wrong with any kitten, or if you are unable to keep them and have no hope of finding them other homes it would be best to cull them soon after birth. In natural conditions many surplus offspring are produced to allow for those that

do not survive and it is foolish to be too sentimental. There is no point in putting yourself to the trouble and their mother to the strain of rearing kittens if they are going to grow up deformed or have to be destroyed a few weeks later because no one wants them. The older they are the more difficult such a decision will be to take. Do not drown kittens; it is a cruel and painful death. Ask your vet for help and at the same time arrange for the mother to be spayed so that no more unwanted litters follow. Do not leave the mother with only one kitten (unless that is all that naturally survives), or she may overproduce milk and develop a mammary disorder. Two kittens will gain a great deal from learning and playing together. While they are still in the nest kittens will learn how to control their limbs and use their senses. They will be able to recognize their mother and their siblings and familiar humans. They will be able to understand their mother's warning of danger and her disciplinary orders. They will be able to crawl, then to walk, even to pounce.

From about three weeks old their mother will begin to leave them for longer periods. The suckling pattern now changes and instead of being initiated by the mother the kittens themselves start demanding milk and if their mother is not there they may climb out of the nest to reach her. Soon these tentative forays become a little longer and their natural excitement and inquisitiveness

will encourage them to explore away from her.

When the kittens are about a month older the mother will spend yet more time away from them. It has been suggested that this is partly because after four weeks nursing her nipples are getting sore, although by now she is down to nursing them for less than five hours a day instead of the fifteen hours or more she put in when they were tiny. Perhaps she is just in need of a rest away from them. Occasionally a nursing cat cannot produce sufficient milk to feed her kittens when they reach this age and they should be encouraged to supplement her supply by lapping the top of bottled cow's milk or undiluted evaporated milk. Soon after they begin to show some interest in solid food; mother may bring a catch home to share with them, or they may try some of her pet food. So the gradual weaning process begins. Milk and a bowl of water should now be available for them, although if they are still getting enough milk from their mother they will not prefer the substitute. Mother will no longer clean up their messes, but will teach them all to use her litter tray.

Playing with each other, and with their indulgent mother who initiates much of the play, kittens learn how to ambush, to catch, to fight and how strong they are and how much energy needs to be put into a particular leap. They continually change roles: the mock predator suddenly becoming the victim, the kitten chased suddenly

chasing back. Many of their actions seem instinctive, but they have to learn both how to coordinate them and for what purpose they can be used. They must practice matching the action to sensory information and to time their reactions to other's movements. Whether they are attacking a brother or sister or trying to catch their mother's flicking tail some instinct curbs any real violence. They soon learn that at the slightest sign of real danger the best course is to disappear!

When they are five or six weeks old outdoor kittens will follow their mother on hunting expeditions, learning all the time from what she does. She will teach them most of what they need to know as cats but this is the time when you should begin to take a hand in their education and start to teach them what they may or may not do as pets according to your household rule book. If you do not want them to get on to certain pieces of furniture stop them now— one of the most difficult things for any young creature to understand is why he is suddenly not allowed to do something which was permitted up until yesterday. Encourage the kittens to use a scratching post instead of digging their claws into your upholstery; when one of them tries to do so simply pick it up and place it by the post which can be a piece of log, an old carpet wrapped around a post, or one bought from a pet shop. Do not let kittens develop a taste for fancy foods. If they turn their noses up at what you offer them

do not leave it down to attract flies and go bad, but do not hesitate
to offer them the same kind of food a few days later. If kittens
do not learn to eat what they are given you will end up with
faddy cats who always expect to dine on luxuries. Experimental
workers claim that training is most effective before kittens are
six weeks old and that later than this it has little permanent effect.
Since some discipline cannot be established until a kitten has moved
to its new home this fortunately does not seem to hold for cats in
a domestic situation but early training is obviously the most
long lasting and it is fortunate that the mother cat includes obedience
to most of the human rules in her own instruction program.
Close association with humans, and especially handling when they
are very young, seems to speed up their physical development.
With this increased stimulation they may open their eyes and
leave the nest earlier than normal. It has even been said that
Siamese cats, which are born white, will develop their colour markings
earlier. Handling, especially by a number of people, may make them
less afraid of strangers and make them more able to cope with
a human environment, but it is also said to reduce the time they spend
in play and to cut down the number of natural contacts they make.
Kittens should not be taken from their mother until they are
eight weeks old and fully weaned. If they are taken from her
earlier they may be emotionally disturbed when adult.

The Friendly Cat

Somehow a traditional view has been established that the cat is a selfish, self-centered animal that has neither loyalty nor affection for others, that it is concerned only with its own affairs and its own advantage. Under natural conditions the cat is a solitary hunter and ungregarious; its physical excellence give it a confidence that discourages dependence and its instinctive caution make it wary of trusting others. The historically brief time it has been domesticated has made little change to its basic character, but the personality of the individual cat will often closely reflect the way in which it has been reared and treated. Although the basic instincts of man show him to be selfish and aggressive, he can nevertheless exhibit consideration and show genuine kindness and concern; so too the cat can be the most attached and affectionate of pets.

The dog is a pack animal and when domesticated tends to behave as though its owner is the leader of its pack, accepting decisions because he has to and eager always to please and to appease to keep his place in the hierarchy. The cat expects a much more democratic attitude. It does not acknowledge any mastery but expects to occupy a negotiated position with recognition of its independence. It does not acknowledge orders, but will accede to requests. It will argue where a dog will plead. It will demand rights and expect privileges where a dog will be happy with almost anything it gets. With a dog man can play the role of a fascist dictator, with a cat he must be egalitarian. A dog could probably survive away from its master but would not from choice seek a life away from home.

A cat can certainly return very easily to a feral life and, if it does not like the home it is offered, may well reject it and seek another, or set up on its own. It choses it be a household cat.

A cat's type, and perhaps to a great extent its particular family line will influence its character and temperament, but the conditions under which it is reared and the environment in which it lives will probably have the most important influence on the kind of pet it is. The closer its pattern of life to that of the wild cat the less involved it is likely to be with its human friends. If a cat can range freely in the countryside chasing its natural prey, is locked out at night and largely ignored except for being fed, it will not become very involved with people. On the other hand, if it is reared from kittenhood in a city apartment with no other animals about, never allowed beyond the door for fear of a traffic accident or theft and forced to rely upon people for food, litter changing and entertainment it will inevitably be very dependent upon human company and if given time and attention will become very closely involved with the humans close to it.

Cats seem to recognize people who have an affinity with them. Many a cat whose owner says "It never likes strangers and usually hides if anybody calls" surprises by making friendly overtures within minutes of this writer's arrival and whether in the middle of the countryside or in a city alley cats will confidently approach to exchange a greeting. Perhaps you too are one of those people whom a cat will cross the road to say hello to, purring and rubbing against your legs, arching its back and lifting its head for you to scratch underneath its chin.

A cat's involvement with a person will be directly related to the attention given to it, and will reflect the nature of that attention. If you put a cat upon a satin cushion with a ribbon around its neck, over feed it and smother it in sentimentality you are likely to end up witth a selfish, lazy and overweight cat. If you lock the cat out at night you will reinforce its natural instinct to be a nocturnal hunter and should not be surprised if it shows up only for meals, spends the daylight hours asleep and sometimes disappears for several days together. If you ignore it for days on end and then expect it to come when called and perform parlor tricks you can hardly be surprised if it displays a total lack of interest. However, if you have

a balanced relationship, remembering that you have a cat and not
a baby or a toy or a piece of decoration for your home, you will find
that you and the cat can rely upon each other and give each other
considerable pleasure. Serve food at regular times and a cat will
turn up for every meal. Consistently reprove a cat for doing something
that you forbid and it will desist (unless it does it just to get
attention or as a display of anger). Show it affection, particularly
by giving it attention, and it will lavish affection back. This will
not just be a matter of cupboard love—although cats, like children,
are often guilty of it—for cats will show both a definite wish
to be with you and to share in your life and considerable concern
if you are for any reason worried or upset. Reject a cat and it will
go off in a huff; go away on holiday without it and it may not
acknowledge you for days when you get back (at least that seems
to be the intention but it may soon betray that it is delighted
to have you back).

It is generally considered that cats are more attached to places
than to people. There are many reports of cats who have been taken
to a new home when the family moved house but who have returned
to their old territory, often finding their way back over considerable
distances. But that is not the whole story.

There are many cats, particularly orientals but all kinds of other
breeds as well, who will pine for an absent human friend and will
consider people much more a center of their lives than any place.
These cats can be travelers too and, while some kind of homing instinct
can perhaps be explained by an orientating sense that enables them
to get back to a location which they know, how can one explain
the phenomenon, also well documented, of cats who, having been left
behind when a family have moved, have searched them out until
they have tracked them down and rejoined them in new territory,
sometimes thousands of miles away?

You would not believe that a New York cat could read the luggage
labels saying that his owner was going to California and then
consult a map to work out how to get there—but that is scarcely less
believable than that a cat could find his owner's new home on the
West Coast after a journey that took five months, as one
New York cat actually did!

Not all cats have to travel so far to find the humans that they love.

Back in the time of Queen Elizabeth I, the Earl of Southampton had a cat which must have been very fond of him for when the earl was imprisoned in the Tower of London for his part in a rising against the queen his cat made its way across London, found a way into the Tower and even discovered Southampton's cell, climbing down the chimney into it. It was a century later before historian Thomas Pennant recorded the story but the earl certainly had his portrait painted with a handsome black and white cat sitting at his elbow and with an inset picture of the Tower of London to give credit to the story.

Another prisoner, Henry Wyatt, incarcerated in that grim fortress by Richard III, was befriended by a cat which came down into the dungeon where he lay without bed, or any covers, and helped him to keep warm, and brought him pigeons she had killed to supplement the meagre food he was permitted. He too was painted with the cat in 1532.

Cats who are close to their humans will often enjoy a trip away from home. If they have confidence in you they take trains, buses and subways in their stride and may thoroughly enjoy a trip by car or taxi. However, do not let your cat out of its traveling basket on transport or in a public place unless it is on a lead. A sudden fright might make it panic or bolt away. Even in a car it is better to keep the cat under restraint so that it cannot interfere with the driver's concentration.

Your cat may happily adjust to living in your vacation home or staying the weekend with friends. However, if it is bad at coming in when called or spends long periods away from home do not risk it failing to return in time to leave when you end your visit. Before planning such a trip make sure that there are no other animals where you are going who might resent, or even attack, a newcomer.

Cats make ideal companions for those people whose circumstances prevent them from being very active. They do not have to be taken out for exercise, they will take it on their own, or even keep

themselves in trim by rushing around indoors. They are fastidiously clean, so are easily trained to use a litter tray if they cannot get outside. They enjoy games that do not demand space or even great activity on the part of their owner. Many people living in small scale accommodation are either young and not earning very much or elderly and living on a pension, so it is an added advantage that cats do not cost a great deal to feed.

It is not only the housebound or the city apartment dweller who will find the cat an ideal pet. Many cats thoroughly enjoy joining their owners on a country walk and a large garden in which to play will make them very happy. They do not require such strict control as dogs and are tolerant of children—who, nonetheless, should be made to understand that animals are not toys. Cats may not, at first, be so tolerant of other animals for they can be very jealous. Occasionally new pets in the house are never properly accepted and the established cat will adopt separate territory to which it withdraws, refusing to have anything to do with the newcomer, but in most cases cats quickly learn to live with other animals. Do not however trust a cat with birds, mice or other natural prey unless it has grown up with them from birth and accepted them as part of its own family —and even then use some sense and do not leave them together unsupervised.

Oriental cats, and some others, especially when housebound, are particularly demanding of attention. They like to be involved in everything that is going on. If allowed to do so they will share your meals, they will sit with you at your desk, join you to watch television, watch you take a bath, sleep on your bed, expect a formal greeting and see you in and out when you leave the house, wake you in the morning if you lie abed, tell you it is time that visitors left

if you are staying up past the time they expect you to turn in and want you to join them in their games. They will argue with you if they disagree, deliberately do something mischievous to attract attention, steal if you give them the opportunity and generally make life more interesting for you and for themselves. Cats do not just sit on the mat unless that is what you want them to do. They can be the liveliest of companions with the added advantage that they are also among the most beautiful.

There are many ways in which cats will demonstrate their affection and show their contentment. A happy cat will often knead a soft surface—a cushion or your jersey—in a gesture which it used as a kitten to pummel its mother's teats and make her milk flow, sometimes dribbling a little at the same time. A happy cat will often roll about and, with a human that it loves and trusts, will roll on its back presenting its stomach to be tickled. They will grip your hand between their front paws, pulling it to them, and kick you with their feet.

Cats not only rub and nuzzle against you to show their affection, they may show it in other ways which other cats would understand and which you should recognize. They may wash you, though less frequently than a dog would and with less slobber. They may gently bite and nip you, or tap you with a paw. They may lick your eyelids or bite your lips to wake you up, and bite your heel or nibble your toes if you go around barefoot—but never so that they hurt, although if you are very ticklish you might have to be more careful at poking a foot out of bed.

Most familiar of all is the happy purr of the cat pleased to see you, a purr which often seems to take on an even deeper note when a cat has the attention of more than one of its favorite people.

The Clever Cat

Cats have an extremely high level of intelligence. Experiments have shown them usually to be more capable of solving complex problems than other animals except for the primates—and they can sometimes do better than monkeys too. Cats have a high learning ability and can be taught to respond to sounds and lights and to avoid unpleasant stimuli, such as electric shocks. They are also able to unlearn an association when circumstances are changed. However, it does not take laboratory tests to prove the cleverness of the cat to a person who owns one.

Of course, it does not do to generalize. There are bright cats and stupid cats, just as there are bright and stupid people. A cat that is clever in one way may not be in another. Just as clever human beings have often exploited those who are a little slower, so you can see one cat in a household taking advantage of another. One bright cat, for instance, would plot how to steal food from the refrigerator and get her stronger and bigger brother to open it by pushing the door in the way she had worked out. If the theft was safely made both had an extra meal—but if she heard someone coming she would rush to meet them with an expression of total innocence, leaving her brother to be caught redpawed. Her owners were not deceived and both got the punishment that they deserved, or at least were blamed where blame was due!

Do cats enjoy pitting their wits against people? They have earned themselves a reputation as skilled thieves, but perhaps it would be more accurate to call them "opportunists" for there is no reason why their actions should coincide with our ideas of right and wrong. Nevertheless, they do appear to take pleasure in outwitting people and seem to enjoy a stolen meal much more than food which is put before them—even to the extent of stealing and eating the same kind of food which they have just refused.

Cats are naturally curious, physically agile and can use their forepaws with great flexibility so that solving physical problems rarely presents them with much difficulty. Yet the male cat mentioned above would often try to open a door that was already ajar by hooking his paw around the door frame instead of around the door. Perhaps this was because this way of opening a door had been demonstrated to him and he had therefore not given the method much attention —cats prefer to learn by observation rather than by demonstration— for he persistently attempted to open doors by reaching up with both paws and trying to turn the door knob, copying the method that he had seen humans use when they opened a door.

To demonstrate another way of thinking altogether, this same cat was not particularly good at catching flies, a sport at which his sister cat excelled. To delude anyone who was watching and save his pride he would chase after a fly and pretend to continue chasing it until he thought it was out of the spectator's sight. Then when the fly settled somewhere and its buzzing stopped, he would make a great show of catching an imaginary fly in his mouth. His disconcerted look when the buzzing started again as the real fly flew away was extremely touching! A failure at dissembling,

this cat nevertheless had an extraordinarily intelligent sensitivity to mood and personality. He would even take sides in human domestic rows and was persistent in offering comfort when his humans were worried or distressed, tolerating their rejection or even violence, if their frustrations were suddenly unleashed at him, with all the patience of a trained psychiatrist.

Most cats are extremely adept at discovering how to operate latches and to use simple physical devices. One, for instance, used to gain immense satisfaction from depressing the foot pedal which operated an electric sewing machine and learned that if the light on the machine was not shining the pedal would not work. But it is not just the extent of a cat's skill which is remarkable, it is a cat's ability

to apply it. To take another example: a young female, having long since discovered that a louvered window could easily be pushed open to allow her to squeeze through, discovered that an upper section with a separate catch was rarely properly shut. Deciding that the edges of the louvers would give sufficient purchase to climb up she balanced, pushed and found her way out—carefully timing this so as to be unobserved by her owner in the garden! Put back indoors, she promptly repeated the escape again for the benefit of the camera.

Tests made with food suspended on a string showed that if something is out of reach and cannot be caught by leaping, or climbing to a point from which it could jump down upon it, a cat was able to realize very rapidly that a box which was placed nearby could be pushed and pulled until it was beneath the string and would then give the cat the necessary extra height to enable it to reach the food quite easily.

In hunting a cat can be observed to chose its moment to attack extremely carefully. If the prey is a dangerous animal, a large rat which could inflict considerable injury, a cat will carefully time its attack so that it leaps upon the rat when it is moving away from it —taking the victim from behind so that it can go straight into the neck bite kill without the rat being able to lash out at it.

Cats are not usually very good at learning tricks, especially when compared with dogs who usually delight in doing so. But that does not mean that dogs are more intelligent—only perhaps that dogs are not so good at thinking for themselves. Cats are quite ready to perform tricks if they are provided with a cooperative and appreciative audience and the tricks are of their own choosing.

Cats like to devise their own performance and to invent their own games and then to invite a human being to cooperate. It is easiest to train a cat in an activity which the cat has already chosen to do: if it jumps up on to your shoulder reward it, and it may do it again. If it likes traveling about in that way it may make it a habit. One thing you should always remember: do not punish a cat for not catching on to what you want or for being uncooperative in this kind of performance. Dogs soon forget a slap—cats may remember forever (and it would probably hurt them more too). Dogs will want to please you, and you will find a pat sufficient reward for most of them. Most cats are more practical and expect a more realistic reward so have a titbit ready.

You will probably find that your cats are too busy training you to allow you time to devise tricks for them. You will find that the basic training necessary to fit a cat into a regular domestic life will demand little effort for it will fit with a cat's own inclinations. Cats are naturally clean and bury their excreta so they will not want to make a mess inside the house. Provide them with a litter tray and they will almost certainly instinctively use it (their mother will probably have trained them very efficiently). If they show any sign of squatting elsewhere pick them up and place them in it, or show them the door if you want them to go outside instead of using

an indoor tray. If they do not cover their mess by pawing litter over it show them by shuffling their paws in the litter. Strangely one blind spot many cats have is that they never appreciate that scraping on the floor outside the litter tray has no effect whatever in covering up their mess. Mother cats often do not realize that shoveling away alongside their kitten does not effectively cover the kitten's droppings. There is more than one instance where a kitten seems to have picked up the wrong idea and continued scrabbling alongside his mess, just like his mother, totally ineffectually, and unable to understand why his nose is still offended by the smell after such effort at burying it. If a cat or kitten has an accident and cannot get to its tray in time or makes the odd mistake, do not punish it and certainly do not rub its nose in the mess it has made, for it will probably be even more upset than you are.

Another thing which few cats seem to understand—although some do pick it up—is the idea of pointing at an object. They tend to concentrate only upon the hand itself. As solitary hunters they do not need to indicate location to other cats in this way, but perhaps if we were able to point our ears as flexibly as the cat we would be able to communicate more easily.

After a time most cat owners find that both they and their cats can communicate a limited range of information, especially requests, demands and thanks. Although some sounds and gestures used with humans recur with many cats they may still be a personal code rather than a definite cat-human "language". Simple means of communication are easily established by being consistent. Teaching a cat to come when called for meals is easy. Just associate the same call, a whistle perhaps, always with food and a cat will soon catch on. Other disciplines are easy to maintain provided that you start when the kitten is very young and do not keep changing your mind about what is allowed. Firm disapproval in your voice is the best admonishment, but avoid using the cat's name or other sounds which you would use when you are pleased with the cat or want it to come to you.

The cat's skill in solving problems can sometimes lead to even greater ones for it does not always see where its action is leading—as when it climbs a ladder or some other height and then has tremendous difficulty getting down again. Humans get into this kind of predicament too. Indeed we are probably much more impetuous, for cats will usually show extreme caution in their investigation of objects or situations. This is not timidity on the part of the cat, for it can show itself among the bravest of animals, but its solitary natural life and total dependence on its own resources have given it a very strong measure of instinctive caution.

The Playful Cat

How playful a cat will be depends upon many factors: its heredity, its rearing, its environment, its opportunities to hunt, its age and, most of all, its own personality and the time which you are prepared to spend with it.

All kittens spend most of their early months playing whenever they are not engaged in the even more important activities of sleeping and eating. They play with their littermates, they play with their mother. When they are taken to a new home they will play with other older cats, with other domestic animals, with humans and by themselves. Play is a vital way of learning many of the skills which they require in adult life.

As a cat grows older and begins to apply its skills to "real" as opposed to play situations it may play less. But since few cats today are dependent upon their own hunting prowess to feed themselves, even their adult hunting may have an element of play and they will have plenty of energy left for activities that are purely pleasurable. The indoor cat relies almost entirely on play to keep itself physically fit and mentally alert and will play much more than the outdoor cat. In its case play is also a major way of filling the boredom of a restricted life.

How boring your cat's life becomes is very much in your control. If it can reach a window with plenty of activity going on outside, a cat will spend many happy hours watching the world pass by. If it has a few simple toys to play with it will play a great deal on its own. If you play with it you can invent innumerable games together. If it has a companion cat they will invent them too. The best plaything for a kitten is another kitten, or failing that a puppy. If carefully introduced most young animals will get on together and older animals will usually accept an infant, even one of another species. There are many dogs that are devoted to their family cat although they would terrorize any other feline they came across. If you do not already have another animal and decide to have a kitten take two not one. If a cat does not have another pet as a playmate it is doubly important that you find time to play with it (and if you say you have not got time then why decide to keep a cat in the first place?).

Some cats will play with anyone—and almost anything; others will play particular games only with particular partners and other games with someone else. Even in a single household you will find games that cats will play together, that they will encourage people to join in, and that each will only play with certain members of the family. You may even have a cat so aware of the correct social balance that it will play alternately with one member of the household and then another.

When it is very young a kitten's games are largely concerned with discovering how to control its body, but as it gets a little older it will begin to play with objects. Sometimes these will be things which can be made to do something and might be called action toys —a ball of wool that can be unrolled, a roll of toilet paper that can be pulled out. More often toys will be objects that can be chased and caught and which serve as substitute prey. Places in which to hide are very popular too and may be as simple as a piece of newspaper to crawl beneath or a cardboard box.

Stuffed toys, often impregnated with catnip, can be obtained from pet shops but they will not necessarily give more delight than a crumpled ball of newspaper, a reel of sewing thread or a piece of string. A ping-pong ball with plenty of bounce in it is usually well-liked. It is too large to be swallowed and too light to chip a tooth (as glass marbles might), but it does have the disadvantage that it cannot be picked up in the mouth or on an extended claw so many cats would prefer an openwork plastic ball. Thin pieces of sponge, the kind used for washing dishes, and similar pieces of scouring cloth, which have been stolen from the kitchen have been a favorite toy with some cats who find them easy to throw all over the place to chase after and catch—but they usually tear them to pieces rapidly and you must keep an eye open to see that they do not swallow the pieces. Certainly a very young kitten should be prevented from playing with them. Similarly young kittens should not be given rubber

or plastic mice for they will usually bite off the tail. If they swallow
a piece of rubber or plastic it could cause a nasty blockage.
Try also to prevent your cat from playing with sharp or very pointed
objects which might injure it and make sure that thread is not left
around with a needle still attached.

Cats, like children, will usually get more fun out of a toy or game
which they have invented for themselves than from any which
have been specially made for them. If you do buy special toys
let the cat discover them and they may prove much more successful.
In addition to balls and other toys which a cat can knock and
throw about, suspended toys will provide animated targets which
it can stretch and jump to catch. Most of all it will enjoy playing
games with things of which you control the movement so a more
competitive element is included. The cat will not expect to win,
playing with you will be much more important to the cat than
being the victor, but let it win at least some of the time.

One of the simplest games consists simply of trailing a piece of string.
Do not just dangle it in the air, drag it along the floor, swirl it
around you, pull it over furniture, through spaces, over you if
you are sitting or lying down. The cat will chase the end, even
if it is watching your hand to see where you are taking it, usually
waiting for the moment before the string disappears from sight
before making its pounce. It will anticipate where it is likely

to appear next, circling around you in the opposite direction to meet it or rushing to the other side of a sofa if that is where you seem to be taking it.

A pen or pencil poked from beneath a cloth or a piece of newspaper and withdrawn to emerge somewhere else makes another favorite target. Anything moving beneath another surface—such as your toes beneath the bedcovers—will be enthusiastically pounced upon. It is not the catching so much as the watching and pouncing that the cat enjoys and it will gladly release something it has caught to have another go. There are all kinds of variations on this kind of pull or push game. One pair of kittens invented their own variation by trying to catch the circle of light from flashlight. If it was switched off they did not scurry around looking for where it had gone but sat still, looking up with a polite but still demanding gaze, and waiting for it to be switched on and for the game to start again.

Cats develop a high degree of control over any kind of small ball. They can dribble one from paw to paw as they rush across the floor in a way that would do credit to an international soccer star. Sometimes they can develop skills in directing it over longer distances, tapping it across a room for someone else to send back to them, but even more they seem to enjoy its random movement, ricocheting off a wall or a chair leg to give them a less predictable target to chase after.

Some cats will invite you to join a game of hide and seek. One neutered tom (whose other favorite game was chasing string) insisted on playing alternately with first his owner hiding and then it being his turn. If he was not rapidly discovered, he would call out to give a clue as to where he was (and usually he was so easy to find that it was a pretense that he had not been discovered) and he expected his owner to do the same. For this cat at least it seemed that being found was the nicest part, not being difficult to discover. Siamese cats in particular seem to enjoy being retrievers and will bring back balls of paper, soft toys or other objects that can easily be carried in the mouth. If they are not thrown far enough away they may knock them further and they seem to take particular delight if the ball can be thrown down stairs to a lower floor. In ancient Egypt wildfowlers trained cats to retrieve birds they had shot, if the evidence of wall paintings is to be believed.

The actions of the cat at play are closely linked to hunting, fighting

and mating behavior. In an earlier chapter you can read about the way in which a cat stalks and pounces on its prey. It uses exactly the same actions when at play stalking a toy, although its final spring is more likely to be a high bound than a frontal spring with its hind feet kept on the ground, for it will not expect the toy to fight back. If a cat has become sufficiently excited it may nevertheless bite a toy as though to kill it, or it may knock it away as sometimes happens with prey, and stalk it once again.

If a cat feels, or has decided to imagine, that a toy is offering any opposition it will grasp it firmly with its forepaws, probably roll over still hanging on to it, and scrabble at it vigorously with both hind feet. These are actions from a typical fight. You can see them carried out in play fights between kittens. They are also performed, as a sign of affection, against a human hand for they have a part in the alternating aggressive and placatory behavior

of a feline courtship. In a real fight the powerful hindlegs would deal savage blows and the claws would be full out trying to slit open the unprotected belly of its opponent.

Cats will often knock playthings underneath low pieces of furniture and then take great pleasure in scooping them out with one paw, a technique used in picking a mouse out of a crevice in which it has hidden. Leaping to catch a dangling object, a cat will spread out its paws and stretch its claws, making a grasping movement which is brought into use when cats are trying to catch a bird as it flies up away from them. It is fascinating to watch a cat's play actions and work out how particular movements and skills would be applied in non-play circumstances.

Whether they are playing with humans or with other cats, an inhibitory mechanism operates to prevent cats doing serious harm, although a sudden shock or surprise in a play situation may momentarily turn a game into a real fight. Aggressive behavior is usually accompanied by some kind of vocalization so you will normally have a warning if a cat thinks that you are being too rough. Nevertheless do not take stupid risks. Do not play fighting games with cats that you do not know very well indeed and when playing with a toy remember that the claws unleashed to catch the toy may scratch you instead—especially if the cat has reached a pitch of excitement or has begun to concentrate on your hand movements rather than those of the other end of the toy. Cats, like children, do get over-excited and forget that they are only playing. They do not mean to hurt you but by then it may be too late.

A cat will be particularly pleased if you play with it on its terms. Although, if you offer to start a game, it may well join in it will be even happier if you join in a game it has initiated—especially if you play like a cat, getting down on the ground to its level. You may not want your neighbors to see you imitating a cat stalking or hiding behind the corner of a sofa, but your cat will find it great fun, especially since it will be so much better at it than you will be.

Since cats are creatures of habit who like regular lives you will find a regular playtime will also be greatly appreciated. Ten minutes when you get in from work or before you go to bed will be something to which both you and your cat can regularly look forward.

You may even find that a particular sequence of games becomes expected. Once the practice has been started it will thereafter be anticipated, so try to set a few minutes aside at the same time every day or you will have a very disappointed cat.

The Inquisitive Cat

"Curiosity killed the cat," says an old proverb, and it is indeed its curiosity which frequently gets it into trouble. For the cat's determination to see what is inside, outside, on top, underneath or wherever is difficult to reach takes it into situations where it may be unable to retrace its steps or exposed to unexpected danger. In these circumstances panic sometimes overcomes a cat's natural caution and exploration ends in disaster. Quite often, however, the danger is in the eyes of the observer. A cat high on the parapet of a building may be quietly concentrating on working out a route for getting down when it finds it is the center of a concentration of excited humans all thinking it is trapped. In trying to escape from them it takes risks that it never would if left alone. How often have firemen been called to "save" a cat "trapped" high in a tree and when the ladders arrive, the cat having lost interest in the view, quietly makes its own way down?

Accidents do happen and cats waking suddenly from sleep on a high ledge or fascinated by watching something outside an open window may forget where they are and fall or make a foolish leap,

but it is extremely rare for a cat to take any reckless action. Their nine lives come not from their fantastic good luck but because their strong sense of self-preservation extracts them from situations that would be the end of less sensible creatures.

Cats like to know what is going on. An interesting noise outside, perhaps an automobile that might be somebody arriving, or footsteps or a voice that attracts attention and a cat may dash to the nearest window. If there are curtains or blinds in the way it will either have a way of slipping through or beneath them to get a better view or may even have learned how to release a venetian blind or window shade to get it out of the way. If there is a comfortable vantage point, a cat may spend hours gazing out, keeping tabs on neighborhood goings on as carefully as any village gossip.

When a cat meets a friendly human or another cat, and especially when one of its own household gets home, it will carry out a detailed olfactory inspection—not to identify them, for it will have done that at a much greater distance, but to determine exactly where they have been and whom they have met from the interesting scents they have brought back upon them.

When investigating new territory indoors a cat will always try to keep an eye on an escape route (outside it can rely on speed to get it into natural cover). If it is with a human who makes it feel secure it may have the confidence to walk boldly into a room but if alone it will be much more cautious. It will not necessarily follow an exact procedure but first will probably listen carefully before putting its head around the door, then it will carefully look around and have a good sniff for any informative scents. Rather than advance into the vulnerable center of the room, it will keep to the sides and the protection of any furniture. When it has decided that all is safe and well it will probably sit down and wash. Investigating objects is carried out just as carefully. First the thing will be carefully watched (usually from cover) to see if it displays any activity. The period of observation gets longer as a kitten grows older and gains in patience. Then the object will be carefully approached, perhaps circled around for a complete visual inspection; next cautiously sniffed, the body held tense and always ready to bound away at the least sign of a dangerous reaction. Now the cat will give it a very fast and very gentle tap with an outstretched foreleg, the paw flexed inwardly, followed perhaps by a rather harder one. If the thing moves, the cat will draw back and watch carefully. Did it move by itself or was the movement simply the result of the blow? Now perhaps it will be time to wash a paw, pretending not to watch—but really noting carefully what happens—and giving time for thought. Next the cat may pull it towards itself, perhaps jumping backwards if very nervous, and if nothing happens may try to turn it over. Then more sniffs, perhaps a lick, even a bite until all the information possible is extracted and the curiosity of the cat is satisfied. The same methods will apply whether the center of interest is a beetle or a boot. If it proves to be something alive, the investigation may repeat the cautious stages every time

the creature moves; if it moves quickly a chase will almost certainly ensue.

Boxes and cupboards—any kind of enclosed space—also seem to cry out for investigation and shopping baskets will be carefully scrutinized to see what you have brought back from the store. Leave a cardboard box on the floor, a cupboard door ajar or a drawer open and a cat delights in jumping inside. This is not so much to find out what is inside, for a cat has probably discovered that before, but because they offer a protected vantage point from which to watch events with a feeling perhaps of the natural cover of a cave or the heart of a bush.

Sometimes a cat will jump in and out of a box with great glee or, if the lid stays in place, will delight in hiding in it and calling out for you to discover where it is. It will thoroughly enjoy hiding under a sheet of newspaper or diving into the concealment of a paper carrier bag.

Heights are something else that no cat seems to be able to resist. Mantlepiece, cupboard, shelf—they will find a way of getting to the highest point that they can to give them a position from which to survey the world. Disciplining them not to jump up on to places you have decreed out of bounds is one of a cat's important early lessons If you are doing some home decorating it is advisable to keep your cat out of the room, for if you leave a ladder or stepladder about it will have climbed to the top the moment that you turn your back, getting in your way, investigating your can

of paint and knocking your tools down on the floor.

Some cats seem to take a deep interest in human correspondence, especially in interrupting it. They will try to catch the flying keys of a typewriter (very dangerous for their paws), grab the end of a pen or pencil and pounce on blobs and blots. They will scrabble through files of papers or pull out letters from a pile on a desk to satisfy their curiosity. Since it always seems to be the very piece of paper that you are looking for that turns up half-chewed on the floor this seems to be more a case of sabotage than of inquisitiveness. If you chide them you will probably receive an appealing look which says either "I was only trying to help" or "Now, will gou give me some attention."

Perhaps these delightfully troublesome cats are careful to choose writers to live with, or perhaps because their humans spend so much time putting marks on paper they develop a fascination for them, but every cat owner will know the way in which the moment that they sit down to read a newspaper or a book their cat seems to be sitting on top of it. Naturally, you say, they want to sit upon your lap and you lift the book out of the way. But no, that is not enough, a paw comes up to stop you reading. You switch the television on and think at least the cat can curl up with you while you watch a program. No, it has left your lap and is sitting on top of the set, swishing its tail right across the picture on the screen. This is not the inquisitive cat but the demanding one who thinks that it deserves all your attention and will not put up with less. Thank goodness that it seems to enjoy listening with you to the radio or the record player.

The Angry Cat

A frightened and angry cat on the attack is a terrifying sight, especially if you are the recipient. Eyes blazing, ears flat against the head and lips pulled back to bare its teeth, with jaws open ready to sink them into you, forepaws outstretched and claws unsheathed and spread, it flings itself at you with incredible speed and force sinking its sharp weaponry into your flesh. Fortunately it is seldom that a cat becomes so enraged and then it will have been provoked by a threat to its own safety that cannot be ignored, and itself in a state of terror, for cats would rather avoid such desperate confrontations.

Cats have developed a very complex system of warnings and attitudes to forestall involvement in a fight and they will put these into operation before launching an attack.

There are three levels of unfriendly behavior: attack, defense and submission. The latter frequently occurs in pack animals, where the animal submitting will have to go on living in the same social group, but is less frequent in the cat. It will appear when a cat accepts that it has done wrong and is frightened that its usual appeal to humans will not gain forgiveness. It also appears when a kitten is accepting the reproof of an adult cat or is seeking to be accepted in a new household. Submission will be shown by the kitten making itself as small as possible and hunching its head into its body; its ears will be kept close to the head but neither erect nor flattened; its eyes may be closed and it will keep quite still.

The most familiar confrontation display seen in the cat is the well-known arched-back which is combined with erect hair, dilated pupils, open mouth and laid back ears, together with stiff legs and a tail either raised erect or slightly to one side. Often the cat will present itself broadside to its opponent, a tactic which can frequently be seen in kitten's play when they approach in a bouncing rush to try to frighten their opponent and retreat as rapidly. Indeed, the broadside attitude is a mixture of aggression and retreat. So too is the arched-back position, for the straight legs and raised tail (the rear part of the cat, and furthest from the enemy) are signals of attack while the erect hair and facial distortion is a defensive reaction. Together the retreating front and advancing rear make the cat arch its spine. Few cats, a nursing female defending her young being the exception, attack from this position, but the appearance of enlarged size can be very intimidating.

Cats can be very jealous and possessive animals. In defense of their rights to territory, property, food or people, cats may be prepared to fight. In the wild, male cats will claim their own territory, a private hunting patch about one tenth of a square mile in area. From this they will seek to exclude other males, although females may be tolerated. They mark their dominion by spraying urine at the boundaries and at particular places such as their favorite claw-sharpening spots, toilet areas, sleeping places and perhaps at mating sites. Females are apparently much less rigidly territorial. In towns and cities it is impossible for a male to claim this kind of territory and they will claim a much more restricted area and

tolerate the right of way of other cats over some of their land. A timetable may even become established as to when each cat has the use of a particular route or path. Favorite spots will still be defended both inside the house and out—this applies equally to female cats and neuters. One may expel all others from a favorite chair, another claim the sole right to sleep upon a bed. The proximity of urban life leads to great friction and greater competition than in the country and there are probably many more fights between cats who would otherwise go no further than a fight display.

Adult cats will use the arched-back threat to dogs, to humans and to some other animals. When two tom cats meet on the edges of their territories or one intrudes upon the territory of another the hunched back and side-on presentation are rarely seen. Their fun rarely stands on end and they usually adopt a crouching stance as though they are about to spring. The two cats will stand quite close together, head to head, emitting deep growls and the rising and falling screams of the angry tom, but they will keep quite still except for the violent swishing of their tails. Very slowly, after perhaps several minutes of inactive confrontation, one of them will begin to edge slowly forward, screaming directly at the other. Suddenly, if there has been no retreat, there will be an explosion of hostility as violent and as fast as a bolt of lightning. If one of them thinks better of it and decides to withdraw he will back away maintaining the attitudes of defensive threat and the other cat will see him off his territory. If a real fight has broken out one tom will probably chase the other until he has taken refuge beyond bounds and ignominiously admitted defeat. If a cat is getting the worst of a fight it will roll on to its back, striking out at its opponent with hind feet as well as forefeet. Because the cat needs to protect its own face, the teeth are used much less than the claws in cat-to-cat fights; few wounds are inflicted by those lethal canines while claw wounds are usually concentrated on the shoulders. Most cat fights sound much worse than they are, but wounds can still be serious and should be carefully tended to prevent the development of infection.

Among cats which live together and to humans a cat will not adopt such drastic measures. It will growl at kittens who try to steal its food or at humans who do something it does not allow. The growl may give way to spitting and the lips will be drawn back to show

the warning flash of teeth. If the transgressor still persists a token blow or a feint in the air may be made, but still the intention to attack will be displayed rather than really carried out, giving the opponent plenty of opportunity to concede and gracefully withdraw. If a cat is frightened of humans because teasing has gone too far or because it finds itself in a strange location, isolated from friends —as for instance when being prodded by the judges at a cat show— it may press itself against the ground in a submissive posture; the tip of its tail will twitch to show annoyance and it will growl. "Stop or I will have to do something nasty," it is saying. If it is still tormented and not allowed to escape it may go into a defensive-submissive attitude, lying half on its side and probably pressing itself against a wall or the side of its cage and may raise an unsheathed paw in a token blow. Then it may roll over to defend itself like a cat who is losing a battle and lash out with all its claws. Often even this action is inhibited with humans and although

the cat may be shrieking with terror and defiance it will not actually lash out.

Kittens playing fighting games may both adopt the sideways arched-back presentation, each reacting to the other as though it were some other kind of animal, but the fight continues more like an actual adult cat fight. The early confrontation is omitted and the two juveniles get to grips clasping each other in their forepaws, rolling and tumbling over and pummelling each other with their hindpaws. They may break their clinch and have a chase: the leading kitten suddenly stopping, as the pursuer gets close, and turning a somersault to bring itself down on its back and under its pursuer in the best position to continue to pound its belly and grip its head with its forepaws. In play these actions are all inhibited from causing serious harm, but the tension of a real fight situation frees these instinctive restraints and they are as savage as the cat can make them.

Turkish Van Cat

Wild
Leopard Cat

The Swimming Cat

Cats are not supposed to like water, indeed a glass of water thrown over them is an extremely effective (and harmless) punishment or deterrent. They will flee if the slightest drop falls upon them. Yet in the area around Lake Van in Turkey there lives a beautiful white and auburn cat that thoroughly enjoys a dip and will swim in the rivers and streams of its homeland.

In fact all cats, and all mammals for that matter, can swim if they have to do so and there is plenty of evidence that they will if it is necessary. Their coat serves as an excellent raincoat, and although they will not relish a thorough drenching they certainly do not mind a shower and may even enjoy being out on a misty day or in a very fine rain, perhaps finding it refreshing as many people do.

They will happily dip a paw into a jug of milk and get it wet. Although they prefer not to walk through a puddle, they certainly do not mind dipping a paw into a bowl of goldfish if they get the chance.

Some cats can become very efficient fishermen. They do not catch fish by swimming in pursuit but scoop them up from the shallows or when they come to the surface near the bank. Wildcats on the coasts of Scotland have become adept at scooping fish out of the sea. According to Dr. Konrad Lorenz, two of the gestures frequently seen used by cats at play are directly linked with their skill as fishermen. Young cats, in particular, will reach beneath a plaything with upturned paws and claws and throw it in a high arc over

their own shoulders, then they will jump after it. This is the way they scoop small fish from the water. With something larger they may sit before it and reach beneath with a paw from either side, then throw it backwards even higher, following it with their eyes and then leaping to where it falls. This is the way, Dr. Lorenz says, in which cats catch larger fish. It has been claimed that big cats in the forests of South America catch fish by dangling their tails in the water like a bait or by flicking the surface of the water with their tails to simulate the action of flies to bring fish to the surface. However, there is no evidence of domestic cats ever using these techniques.

Whether they are fisher cats or not, many household pets love playing with water. They will watch the water running from a faucet for ages and will try to catch the droplets from a faucet that drips. Some pets enjoy sharing bathtime with their humans and will join them—sitting on the edge. They would not be so happy should they fall in for, except for the Turkish Van, cats do not usually enjoy being given a bath. When they get wet cats have to lick themselves dry so if you do have to wash them or they get soaked in a downpour give them a brisk rub with a rough towel and then a vigorous brushing to help them dry out. They may object at first, so wrap them well up in the towel, but when the brushing starts they will begin to appreciate your attention.

Cats must have water to drink, even if they take plenty of milk, and a fresh supply should always be put down for them. Equally they may always ignore it and insist on drinking water from some other source. Perhaps the water from a puddle tastes better than that which runs through a faucet after being processed through the waterworks. Cats can be very discriminating: they can also be plain cussed!

If you own a cat you will have recognized many features of its behavior in these pages, and at other times have noticed cases where your cat adopts a different approach to living. Some of a cat's behavior is predictable but it is its individuality and variety that give each cat its personality.

Acknowledgements

The publisher would like to thank the following for supplying the photographs reproduced in this book:

C. Adriaanse page 19; Elly Bientema page 18, 21, 32, 35*t*, 35*c*, 35*b*, 58, 59*b*, 64; Anne Cumbers page 9*t*, 10*tl*, 10*tr*, 15, 41, 46*tl*, 51, 52*t*, 52*b*, 52*r*, 53*t*, 53*c*, 53*b*, 54*t*, 57, 59*t*, 62, 67*t*, 71, 78*b*, 79*t*, 81*t*, 82, 85, 87*b*, 90*c*, 90*bl*, 90*br*, 94*tl*, 94*bl*, 95; Robert Estall page 20*t*, 23*b*, 29, 34*tr*, 40, 46*bl*, 67*b*, 84*b*, 96; Paul Forrester page 13, 20*b*, 22*b*, 26-27, 33, 36*b*, 38*t*, 43*r*, 47*tr*, 60, 63*tl*, 63*tr*, 63*b*, 66*b*, 70*t*, 70*b*, 72*t*, 79*b*, 86*t*, 87*t*, 91*t*; Sonia Halliday page 10*b*, 92*t*; Geoffrey Kinns (Natural Science Photographs) page 8*t*; Howard Loxton page 1, 2-3, 14*b*, 16-17, 28*b*, 44-45, 56*t*, 56*b*, 73, 89*t*, 89*b*, 94*tr*; John Moss page 43*t*, 65*bl*, 72*t*; Peter Myers page 46*br*;

Spectrum Colour Library page 7, 12*br*, 12*bl*, 14*t*, 23*t*, 25*t*, 31*b*, 34*tl*, 36*t*, 37*b*, 42*b*, 47*br*, 54*b*, 55, 76, 78*t*, 80, 81*c*, 81*b*, 90*t*, 91*b*, 92*b*; G. Stoscheck page 9*b*; Sally-Anne Thompson page 8*b*, 11, 22*t*, 24*b*, 30*t*, 30*b*, 31*t*, 37*t*, 39, 42*t*, 43*cl*, 43*bl*, 61, 65*t*, 83, 84*t*; Norman Tozer page 69; ZEFA page 6, 12*t*, 24*t*, 34*b*, 38*b*, 47*l*, 68, 86*b*, 93, jacket; ZEFA/Photri page 66*t*; ZEFA/Photri/Johnson page 5; ZEFA/Photri/Lani page 25*b*, 50*t*, 50*b*; ZEFA/Photri/Spies page 28*t*, 48-9, 65*br*, 74-75, 77, 88.

The Publishers have attempted to observe the legal requirements with respect to the rights of the suppliers of photographic materials. Nevertheless, persons who have claims are invited to apply to the Publishers.